The feckin' book of Irish Stuff: Céilís, Claddagh Rings, Leprechauns and other aul' Blarney.

Colin Murphy & Donal O'Dea

THE O'BRIEN PRESS
DUBLIN

The Aran Sweater

The Aran Sweater is internationally renowned as the symbol of two things: The Aran Islands and tourists with wojus fashion sense. It was said that the original hand-knitted patterns in the wool were so unique that in the event of the fisherman wearing it being drowned, the body could be identified from his sweater. This is ironic, really, as no Irish person nowadays would be seen dead wearing one.

The basket-stitch in the sweaters represents a fisherman's basket, expressing a wish for a hopeful catch, and today the catch comes in the form of unwary visitors to our shores who are charmed into parting with a gansey-load of money for their bit of genuine Aran Island heritage, which was most likely made by a machine in Indonesia.

B & B

The B&B sign is part of the Irish landscape, as familiar to Irish people the world over as the sight of burnt-out cars in beauty spots and crisp packets in hedges.

The origins of the B&B name go back to the days of sexual repression in Ireland (5000BC – AD1990), when these country homes became a refuge for courting couples eager for privacy where they could indulge in some illicit shenanigans far from the prying eyes of parents or priests.

This is where the term B&B sprang from, which every Irish person over thirty knows means 'Bed & Bonk'.

Begorrah

Begorrah is an expression of surprise or shock used only by stereotypical Irish characters in American movies. The chances of actually hearing it from a real Irish person are as remote as those of finding a banking official in Ireland with a clear conscience. Apparently it originated in the mid-nineteenth century and derives from 'by God'. Say 'by God' when you're gee-eyed drunk, and it will probably sound like 'begggorrrrahhhh'. In Hollywood, however, especially up until recent years, every Irish person used the word in every sentence. A typical scene would go something like this:

Irish Stereotype 1:

> *'Top of the mornin', Officer O'Shaughnessey, faith and begorrah.'*

Irish Stereotype 2:

> *'Begorrah it is to be shure, Mickaleen. So anyway, begorrah and bejapers, why, begorrah, did you chop up yer poor sainted wife Maureen with an axe?'*

 The Blarney Stone

Kissing the Blarney Stone supposedly bestows 'the gift of the gab', or eloquence in speech. Stroll down any Irish street on a Friday night and simply listen to the pearls of oratory flowing from our lips:

> 'Howaya Mick, yebollixye.'
> 'How's she cuttin', Fiona?'
> 'Ah I'm rat-arsed, I am.'
> 'Yeah? So any chance of a ride?'

From these gems of dialogue we can quickly surmise that few Irish people have ever kissed the Blarney Stone.

Legend has it that Cormac McCarthy, Earl of Blarney, was asked for his loyalty by Queen Elizabeth I and his reply was so florid that nobody knew whether he'd said yes or no. Nearly half a million tourists kiss the stone each year in Blarney Castle, which involves lying flat on your back and bending over arse-ways above a vertigo-inducing drop.

The website TripAdvisor recently labelled the Blarney Stone 'the most unhygienic tourist attraction in the world'.

HORRACE HONEY, ARE YOU SURE THAT THIS IS THE WAY THE GUIDE SAID TO KISS THE STONE?

The Bodhrán

This is the hand-held drum-like instrument that is traditionally used to keep time to a bunch of trad Irish music performers getting langered in the pub. Every rapid-fire beat of the bodhrán must be accompanied by someone taking a mouthful of stout. The success of the technique can easily be measured by the increasing frequency with which the other musicians and audience shout things like 'yehooo' or 'yupthereyeboyye'.

The bodhrán itself is made from a goatskin stretched across a circular wooden frame, appropriately enough, as the audience usually gets so plastered they often end up stretched unconscious across the nearest table.

The World Bodhrán Championships are held in Milltown, Co Kerry every year. Individual competitions include 'Throwing your bodhrán at a cow in a field', 'Drinking a bodhrán full of stout', and everyone's favourite, 'The international topless bodhrán race.'

The Book of Kells

This is often described as Ireland's most valuable national treasure, after U2 that is, who bring in a lot more much-needed tax revenue. It is an elaborately decorated, intricately crafted version of the Four Gospels which was created by Irish monks on the Scottish Island of Iona, but who had to leg it back to the Abbey of Kells around AD800 as Viking raiders kept turning up and kicking the living shite out of them.

The masterpiece took yonks to knock together and the unfortunate monks often got bored working on it. We know this because they left notes in the margins, like: 'I've a pain in me bleedin' hole doing this.'

The pages were made from the skins of 200 cows and the ink came from a mixture of soot and fruit juice, much like any popular brand of sports drink today.

The book is now kept in Trinity College, Dublin and, along with the P45, is the only document in Ireland seen by half a million people every year.

Céad Míle Fáilte

For those not versed in the Irish language, this translates as 'a hundred thousand welcomes.'

As there are approximately four million people in Ireland, this means that if you are a visitor, the chances of you getting a warm welcome are approximately one in forty.

Just kidding. Almost every single Irish person you encounter will be only too happy to extend a warm and welcoming hand to you, the visitor, as, besides us being a naturally friendly and hospitable lot, you have something we need desperately right now: Money.

Céad míle fáilte to Ireland.

Céilís

Before discos and nightclubs, the céilí dance was the traditional way for Irish people to get off with each other and hopefully end up with a snog and a grope in a dark alleyway. Unlike nightclub dances, which involve prancing about like a goat with its arse on fire to eardrum-bursting music, the céilí involves prancing about like a goat with its arse on fire to eardrum-bursting Irish dance music.

Céilís are still popular in small Irish towns and are usually held in school halls, sports clubs, living rooms, cowsheds, outside toilets and the back of small vans. The main type of

dance is called a set dance. This involves four couples, with each pair opposite another pair in a rectangle; each couple exchanges positions with the facing couple and the facing couples exchange partners, not dissimilar to the sort of thing that happens at a swingers' party. In fact, among the names of popular céilí dances are 'The Sausage Machine', 'Strip the Willow' and 'The Swedish Masquerade', or are they what happens in the laneway behind the hall when the céilí is over?

The Celtic Tiger

Remember this? Ha ha, what a feckin' gas. The reality is that there never was a boom in Ireland, there was just a wojus big borrowing spree. Everything we had turns out to have been bought on the never-never. And now it's payback time.

We weren't actually *making* anything during the Celtic Tiger years, like tables or tins of beans or saucepans or bicycles. Instead, all we were doing was building over-priced houses, which we couldn't afford to pay for because we didn't give a shite about industries making tables or tins of beans or saucepans or bicycles. Why are we so surprised that our economy is banjaxed?

Still, look at what we have to show for the Celtic Tiger 'boom': 300km of motorway, which cost approximately a million euro a centimetre to build.

Never mind, if we all start saving now we should have our debt paid off in time for the 200th anniversary of the Easter Rising.

THE NEW SYMBOL
OF THE IRISH ECONOMY
'THE CELTIC SLOTH'

The Claddagh Ring

This is one of the handiest gadgets we Irish ever invented.

It consists of a ring with two hands clasping a heart with a crown on top (meaning some oul' guff like 'let love and friendship reign forever').

If you're a male eyeing up a bit of skirt, you can tell if you've any chance of getting her in the scratcher by having a gander at her Claddagh ring. If she's wearing the ring on her right hand with the heart facing out, there's a chance of getting your leg over. If you're a mot who's 'in love' already, you can ward off the randy bowsie that's leering at your boobs by displaying your Claddagh on your right hand with the heart facing inwards, letting him

know you're romantically involved and that your boyfriend is about to arrive and beat the living crap out of him. If the girl is wearing the ring on her left hand, she's definitely hitched and probably has three kids, a mortgage and stretch marks.

Of course, if everyone's gee-eyed, all bets are off…

 ## Colleen

The traditional image of the Irish colleen was perpetuated not just by the usual overseas stereotypers, but by the likes of Dev himself and by the early Irish Tourist Board, who portrayed her on posters and on postcards as a flaming red-haired beauty dressed in a traditional green costume, complete with shawl, often carrying a bunch of shamrock and standing against a green flag bearing a golden harp. She is the embodiment of virtue, holiness and innocence.

The modern image of the Irish colleen has changed a little, as she now has bleached hair, a nose ring and wears a white skirt that comes halfway up her arse. She carries a bottle of vodka in one hand and a fag in the other and is always on the lookout for some 'rides', especially after she gets rat-arsed. Ah, sure she'd put de heart cross-ways in ye.

Comely maidens dancing at the crossroads

This phrase has been attributed to former president Eamon de Valera, as part of his vision for Ireland. In fact, the poor fecker never actually said it.

The only reference to maidens in his 1943 speech was: '… a land whose countryside would be bright with … the contest of athletic youths and the laughter of happy maidens…'

Some gobshite hack invented the 'comely maidens' line and poor Dev has been stuck with it ever since.

Connemara Marble

The world's only green marble, Connemara marble was used in ancient times to make spearheads, jewellery, rosary beads, crosses and even as a form of currency. As Ireland is now broke, this latter use is being reconsidered, and one kilogram of the shiny green stone will buy you a 50% shareholding in any of Ireland's major banks.

In the Sixties and Seventies, every Irish mantelpiece was adorned with all sorts of ganky ornaments made from Connemara marble… leprechauns, shamrocks, Celtic crosses, cats, dogs, hippos, various sex toys etc.

Its rich emerald tones have also made it popular as jewellery and it can be worn as a necklace, a bracelet, a wedding ring, and as earrings, eyebrow rings, nose rings and nipple rings.

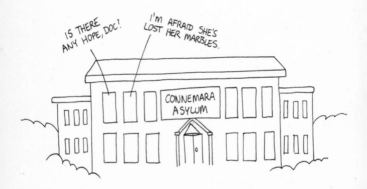

Connemara Pony

The Connemara Pony is a world-famous
breed, known for their fine disposition
and athleticism. They used to feature a
lot in John Hinde postcards in the Sixties
(see *John Hinde Postcards*), mainly because the
people in Connemara were too bleedin' ugly to
photograph.

Legend has it that when the Spanish Armada
ran aground on the Connemara coast in 1588,
a bunch of Andalusians were set loose and
quickly began to mate enthusiastically with the
local stock. It's also said that the Andalusian
horses did the same.

Craic

This is a uniquely Irish phenomenon, and can only be fully understood and appreciated by Irish people. It is probably the most sought-after commodity in Ireland, taking precedence over money, career, marriage, family and religion.

If you're a foreigner reading this, *craic* loosely translated means 'fun', but is much more complex than that. Whereas, for example, the English idea of having fun involves either staring silently at each other

RIGHT, TAOISEACH, WE'RE AGREED THAT WE NEED TO BORROW €87 BILLION. NOW LET'S LEG IT TO THE PUB FOR A BIT OF CRAIC.

CABINET ROOM

over piss-weak English ale for hours on end or getting rat-arsed and ranting Ye-wah! Ye-Wah! Ye-Wah', Irish craic involves multi-layered social interaction that incorporates talking, drinking, laughing, gossiping, more drinking, slagging and trying to get off with some young-wan or youngfella.

Craic can be expressed in many ways, eg 'The craic', 'What's the craic?', 'It was great craic!' and lots more.

American and British visitors are frequently shocked when they misinterpret an Irish guy casually inquiring of an Irish girl 'How's the craic?'

 # Cronyism

You might be surprised that we didn't invent cronyism, but in the same way that Brazilians and Italians didn't invent soccer but are now masters of the sport, Ireland is the unofficial world champion of cronyism. And our Pele of Cronyism is a well-known political party.

Cronyism in Ireland works like this:

Mick the Builder:
> *'Howaya Minister, what'll it be?*

Minister:

> 'A pint, Mick, and a large contribution to party coffers. How's the wife and kids?'

Mick the Builder:

> 'They're grand, Minister. So, wouldn't it be great if that new road-building budget was spent in Offaly?'

Minister:

> 'Ah, it would, Mick, but they need the roads more in Mayo.'

Mick the Builder:

> 'There's your pint. Oh, what's that? Look, you dropped that brown envelope on the floor.'

Minister:

> 'Oh, yeah, I did, didn't I? Well, here's to you, Mick. And may the Offaly road rise up to meet ye.'

Which is why Ireland lags a country mile behind the rest of the developed world in *everything*.

The Currach

You can't miss the currachs in the west of Ireland, as they're dangling from the ceiling of every second pub. In the old days they were made from animal skins stretched over a wooden frame, but nowadays they use empty plastic peat moss sacks.

They were once used for fishing and taking your mot for a court on the ocean, giving rise to the expression 'riding the waves'.

JAYSUS, MICK, I'VE HAD ENOUGH OF YOUR PENNY-PINCHING. TOMORROW I'M GOING TO GALWAY AND BUYING MYSELF AN UMBRELLA

AH NO, MICK, SURE I'm STILL IN BALLYDEHOB DESPERATELY TRYIN' TE SCRAPE A FEW SHILLINGS TOGETHER...

Cute Hoor

These slimy individuals inhabit all walks of Irish life, but the best-known are affluent members of certain political parties, senior civil servants, successful building contractors, rich tax evaders etc. They pass themselves off as innocent, poverty-stricken Holy Joes, while in reality the sly bowsies would shite in your parlour and charge you for it. This particular type of sleeveen generally blames someone else when they banjax something and is then capable of putting on a face as innocent as a baby's when it farts.

The one thing about cute hoors is that they are generally easy to spot. They have an overly friendly manner, are as tight as a camel's arse in a sandstorm and they have a neck like a jockey's bollix.

Many people believed that the demise of the Celtic Tiger years would see a decline in the species. But as another Irish politician said in a different context, 'They haven't gone away, you know.' Watch your wallets.

Direction Road Signs

The traditional Irish road signs with raised black lettering on a white background are beginning to vanish from Irish roads, mainly because publicans steal them to use as ornaments in their pubs.

Most of these signs were erected in the Forties and Fifties and they all had two things in common – they pointed in the wrong direction and the distances indicated on them were a load of shite. In fact, they were about as

ARE YOU SURE YOU WANT TO MAKE THIS DIVERSION, DUCHESS?

MOUNTCHARLES

useful as a one-legged man in an arse-kicking contest.

For some reason the most sought-after sign is for Muff on the coast of Donegal, where they have a Diving club. *They do. Really.*

The Dolmen

All around Ireland you will find examples of massive constructions in remote, godforsaken areas, the purpose of which little or nothing is known. They're called Ghost Housing Estates.

Pre-dating these by about 6000 years are the dolmens, which were burial sites. Unlike modern building techniques, which involve nailing a few sheets of plasterboard together and calling it a wall, the dolmens required our

UNFORTUNATELY THERE WERE TWELVE GUYS CRUSHED WHEN THE STONE COLLAPSED.

AH JAYSUS! YOU MEAN WE HAVE TO BUILD TWELVE MORE OF THESE BLEEDIN' THINGS?

prehistoric ancestors to somehow raise a giant rock, weighing up to 100 tons, on top of three other upright giant stones. Construction would have involved about a thousand men, tons of machinery and required an enormous logistical operation, just like an Irish county council fixing a burst water pipe.

The Drunken Irishman

The stereotype of the Irishman (or woman) with which we're all so familiar from movies and TV: the rat-arsed, usually genial Irish guy staggering around making a gobshite of himself under the disgusted or amused eyes of everyone else, probably singing something like 'Oooh Dannnyyyy booooyyy… de pipes de pipes arrreee calllllinnnnn'.

Although we've encountered this poor gobdaw in countless Hollywood movies, it was actually the Brits who invented the stereotype. They did this because any self-respecting Irishman can drink any pansy Brit under the table (three pints and they're paralytic), so the poor eejits had to cover their wimpiness by feigning abhorrence at Irish people's capacity for alcohol.

Unfortunately, the truth nowadays is that life is beginning to imitate the stereotype, as Ireland has recently come first in the European league of binge drinkers. Well, you know what they say, if you want to be good at anything, practise, practise, practise.

The Easter Rising

The bit of history the Christian Brothers used to love batin' into everyone, about how our boys Pearse, Connolly etc sacrificed themselves to show the world what a bunch of bloodthirsty scumbags the Brits were. At least that was the version we all learned, with Pearse staring down at us from the classroom wall.

One thing is for certain, Easter Monday 1916 was a lousy day to pick to go and collect your pension at the GPO or to go Boland's factory to buy a pack of fig rolls. One way or the other it did spell the beginning of the end for the Brits in Ireland as, true to form, they created a whole new generation of martyrs. We'll be celebrating the centenary of the leaders' sacrifice in a few years time by wearing plastic leprechaun hats and getting drunk while our crooked politicians watch on as they're entertained by their cronies and cute hoors. Maybe we should have let the Brits keep the place.

The Full Irish Breakfast

The summit of Irish culinary arts, after a week of eating these, your arse will be as wide as a Leitrim hurler's shot. The 'Full Irish' consists of the following: two slices bacon (preferably streaky), two sausages, one fried egg, one slice black pudding, one slice white pudding, one Irish potato cake, fried mushrooms, one fried tomato, fried bread, heavily buttered toast and Irish soda bread. (Please note: bacon, sausages, eggs etc should be fried in butter.)

The mere sight of the 'Full Irish' has been known to frighten the shite out of visiting heart surgeons, dieticians and vegetarians. Although slower than a Smith & Wesson, it can kill just as effectively if consumed on a regular basis.

In fact, in every sense, the Full Irish Breakfast is deadly.

HERE LIES FRANK. TAKEN FROM THIS EARTH BY THE IRISH BREAKFAST ~2011~

The Harp

Along with the plastic bag in the tree and the burnt-out car in the beauty spot, the harp is the official national symbol.

The harp that you see on your Euros, passport, state documents etc is a left-facing image, (taken in 1922) of Brian Boru's harp, which you'll find in Trinity College, and is nearly as old as poor ould 'axe-in-the-back' Brian himself. The reason it's a left-facing image is that Guinness had already snapped the right-facing image of the same harp and registered it as a trademark in 1862. Now there's something to bore the arse off your pals with next time you're in the pub.

The harp is also the official seal of the President. Rumour has it that the President keeps the unofficial seal in a pond in the back garden of Áras an Uachtaráin.

The High Cross

The High Cross is another example of Insular Art (see *The Book of Kells*) from a time in the distant past when Ireland was known as the Land of Saints and Scholars. Nowadays it is known primarily as the Land of De-frocked Priests and Swindlers.

The High Cross is a monumental work of highly decorated stone with a ring encircling the cross-piece. They are considered priceless and Ireland is currently trying to flog them to pay off our national debt, which is monumental in itself.

The most famous example is found at Monasterboice, known as Muiredach's High Cross and is thought to be over a thousand years old. Much more recently, during the Jack Charlton era, the Ireland manager re-introduced 'the High Cross' towards Niall Quinn's head as the team's only means of attack.

Hooley

One theory about the word 'hooley' is that there was once a rowdy Irish gouger and thief by the name of Hooligan who lived in England and who liked to throw wild parties where all sorts of immoral shenanigans went on.

The hooley is somewhat of a dying tradition in Ireland, the music, feasting, courting, story-telling and drinking having been replaced with just the drinking. Yet most people can still remember there being a hooley in their home: fifty people squashed into a living room designed for ten, everyone langered, plates of cheese and pickled onions on cocktail sticks being passed around; everyone doing their party piece, which could be a song, a story, a joke or anything you fancy, but was usually 'Danny Boy' sung to the tune of 'The Wild Rover' in between slurps from a pint bottle of Guinness.

All songs, it seemed, had to end with the obligatory 'Eyeeeee luvvvvvv yeeeuuuuuu'.

Hurley

Genuine hurleys are made only from ash wood, but in the Seventies there was a brief flirtation with making them from plastic. When it was realized that these were more likely to cause serious injury, there was a massive surge in demand, but eventually they were banned.

WE'RE BEING INVADED! QUICK. BREAK OUT THE HURLEYS!

Hurleys have been around for millennia and, in fact, even appear in Irish legend, when, as a young boy, Cúchulainn slew the Hound of Culain by belting a sliotar down its gob with his hurley. The legend is celebrated in thousands of hurling matches every week when the two teams try to do precisely the same to each other.

Serious hurlers wrap metal bands around the *bas* of their hurleys, both to reinforce the wood and because the metal can reef lumps of flesh off an opponent's body. It is not uncommon for a hurler to go through several hurleys in a single game as they can easily break when they collide with an opposing player's head.

Irish Coffee

Back in the early Forties, Foynes in Limerick was one of the world's aviation hubs. 'Foynes?' you say. 'Is yer man a few pints short of a milk churn, or wha?' It's true, as Foynes was the re-fuelling point for most US seaplanes. Now, travelling on these planes was cold enough to freeze the gee off a slapper, and one night in 1942, when a bunch of shivering passengers landed on a Pan Am flight, the head chef at Foynes, Joseph Sheridan, had the idea of adding Irish whiskey to the coffee to warm them up, telling the grateful Yanks that this was called 'Irish coffee'.

A travel writer called Stanton Delaplane experienced Irish coffee at Shannon in the Fifties and brought it back to the US, where he and a couple of friends spent an evening sampling the coffee and getting completely plastered. He then promoted the coffee in the

HOW DO WE TURN THIS COUNTRY INTO A VIABLE TOURIST DESTINATION?

LET'S SPIKE THE COFFEE!

TOURISM INNOVATION FORUM 1942

Buena Vista Café in San Francisco and wrote about it in his columns, making it famous everywhere from Ballygobackwards to Berlin to Boston.

To make it properly, you need fresh, hot coffee with brown sugar, add a measure of Irish whiskey and then slowly pour fresh cream over the back of a spoon so that it sits on the surface of the coffee and doesn't sink. Irish Coffee is guaranteed to warm the cockles of your heart, not to mention the cockles in all your other body parts.

Irish Dancing

Irish Dancing is divided into two distinct types, social dancing (see *Céilís*) and performance dancing, which is what inspired Riverdance, for which the world will never forgive us.

Stepdancing involves keeping your upper body and arms rigid, as though you were dead from the waist up, then kicking your knees up and down like the bejaysus until you collapse from exhaustion.

There are two categories of stepdance – soft shoe and hard shoe. Soft shoe dances include the reel, slip jig, single jig, light jig, heavy jig and the extremely heavy jig, which is only performed by fat people. Hard shoe dances

include the hornpipe, the treble reel and the hard jig, so-called as it's a pain in the bollox trying to learn it.

Irish dancing costumes traditionally involve extremely short dresses decorated with lace, sequins, Celtic embroidery and feathers. And that's just the men.

Irish Fairies

Otherwise known as 'the little people', 'the wee folk' and by various other nicknames, there are actually Irish people alive today who still believe in fairies. Granted, most of these people also believe Westlife are the greatest band in history, that the Dublin Metro will be built and that bank officials are honest people.

Just in case these gobshites are right, here's some stuff you should know. The favourite gathering place of the fairies is the hawthorn tree, so if you live near one, burn it to the ground immediately. Never build a house on a fairy path, as this really pisses them off and they will curse everyone within to eternal stupidity, as happened with Leinster House.

If you offend a fairy they will strike you with a Fairy Dart, usually in the arse, which causes

severe swelling. This seems to have happened to a great number of the Irish population in recent years, as about one third of us have arses the width of a small car.

Another well-known fairy ailment is the Fairy Stroke. This is when a fairy arranges for planning permission for a house, in breach of zoning regulations, in return for a pot of gold.

Irish Fiddle

Apparently there is no difference between a violin and an Irish fiddle, except that the former produces a musical sound and the latter a noise like a bunch of cats on a bonfire. Alternatively, if you can imagine the theme music from *Psycho* being played like the clappers, and by three different people, all out of harmony, you get a good idea of what an Irish fiddle sounds like.

The fiddle has been a key component of Irish music for over 200 years, one of the other key components being getting completely locked.

There is a gansey-load of different traditions of fiddling, like Donegal fiddling, Sligo fiddling, Clare fiddling or general Irish fiddling, such as when a county councillor fills out his expenses sheet.

Irish Jarvey

Irish Jarveys,
(who are mainly
based in Killarney)
traditionally drive
jaunting cars with
the seats running
lengthwise so
the passengers
sit with their
backs to each
other. This is so
there can be no
illicit acting the
maggot going on

SERIOUSLY, LAD
DO YOU MIND?

between a courting couple behind the driver's
back (as in *The Quiet Man*) and also to allow
you to enjoy the views of all the fast food
restaurants and pound shops in Killarney.

In recent times the jarveys have been in
dispute with the National Park and Wildlife
Service. In fact, the shit hit the fan, or to be
more accurate, it hit the road. The NPWS
insisted that the jarveys use dung-catchers
to stop them covering the scenic roads in
Killarney National Park with crap, or rather

to stop the jarveys' horses covering the roads with crap. The jarveys insisted that these made the horses uncomfortable – and if you don't believe them, you try walking around for ten hours with a bag attached to your arse.

The jarveys have been taking tourists for a spin around the Lakes of Killarney for over a century, and as they'll tell anyone who inquires about the dispute: 'Ara bejaysus, shit happens.'

Irish Mammy

Fancy a nice cup of tea in bed the night after you've been on the lash, spilled a pint on your trousers, dropped your pizza face down on the kitchen floor when you got home and left

AH, WOULD YOU LOOK AT HIM THERE, ASLEEP SUCKING HIS THUMB. WHAT AGE IS HE?

THIRTY-FOUR.

your alcohol-soaked underpants hanging from one of the fridge magnets?

Well, uniquely in the world, only the Irish Mammy will happily bring you one.

She'll iron your socks, make you rasher sandwiches, boil your underwear in a pot, sterilize your sheets and burst the pimple on the spot you can't reach, and all the while tell the neighbours what a treasure you are. And, also uniquely in Ireland, she'll do all this until you're well into your thirties or beyond. In fact, if you get married, she'll worry herself sick that your wife isn't doing precisely the same.

 Irish Priest

The Irish priest in Ireland's collective memory conjures up two totally divergent images, one of which has come about mostly in recent decades. There is the lovable Bing Crosby or Barry Fitzgerald-type priest, who enjoyed a drink or two with the lads, would gently counsel colleens on the virtues of virginity, offer comfort to a distraught mother whose eight sons had just been executed by the

British, and sprinkle his sermons with amusing hurling metaphors.

Then there is the priest who beats the crap out of orphans with leather straps and wooden rulers, is guilty of all sorts of unmentionable crimes of abuse and yet harangues his flock with puritanical rants about the evils of sex, violence, drunkenness, sex, and more sex. Come back, Barry Fitzgerald, all is forgiven.

BLESS ME FATHER, FOR I HAVE SINNED.

Irish Pub

The single greatest achievement in the history of mankind. Well, at least until the gobshites decided to introduce a draconian smoking ban, almost rendering all Irish pubs both smoke and customer-free. Until that tragic day in 2003, people could go on the batter to their favourite pub for hours on end, joyfully soaking up the booze, the treacle-thick atmosphere of cigarette fumes and as much craic and gossip as they could digest. Truly wonderful places.

Nowadays the bars and lounges of most Irish pubs are as deserted as the Dáil chamber on payoff day. Tumbleweed bobs lazily through the void that once echoed to the sound of happy, gee-eyed conversation between biffos and buckos, slappers and scangers, geebags and gobdaws. Head-the-balls got off with muck savages, dossers snogged wagons and jackeens shared a joke with mulchies. The Irish pub used to be a true microcosm of Irish life, or at least Irish life when it was pissed.

Unfortunately, our nanny Government told us that they knew better. Should be feckin' barred.

Irish Stew

The ingredients for a genuine, traditional Irish stew include mutton, potatoes, onions, carrots, parsley, turnip, cabbage, some old boot laces (finely chopped), the remains of the pizza your had last Wednesday week, a lump of moldy bread and whatever else you can sweep up off your kitchen floor, (the purists tell us that the carrots are optional). Boil all this for four hours. Add salt and pepper.

It may be cheap, it may be unpleasant to look at, it may smell like a sock you found under the bed, but, by Jaysus, it's fierce stuff altogether for curing a hangover.

EAT YOUR HEART OUT GORDON RAMSAY.

Irish Whiskey

Scotch is the most popular whisky in the world, which just shows you what an ignorant bunch of gobshites the rest of the world is. Real whiskey (with an 'e'), as any self-respecting boozer can tell you, comes from Ireland. The Scots were still in caves grunting at each other when we invented the word whiskey – it comes from the ancient Gaelic *'uisce beatha'*, meaning the water of life.

Unlike Scotch, which is only distilled twice, Irish whiskey is always triple distilled. And because the eejits across the water use peat in the malting process, it gives Scotch what they call an 'earthy' flavour i.e. it tastes like earth mixed with nettles. Irish whiskey, on the other hand, is infinitely smoother on the tongue, and won't strip the lining off your guts like its Scottish paint-stripper equivalent.

On top of all that, Irish whiskey is the earliest distilled drink in Europe (12th century), and the Bushmills Distillery in Antrim is the oldest distillery in the world (1608).

So stick all that up yer kilts! Irish Whiskey *go bragh*!

It's a Long Way to Tipperary

One of the best-known Irish ballads in the world, which is a bit of a pain in the arse, as it's actually British. It was written by Jack Judge who was from Manchester, although his parents were Irish and his grandparents were from Tipp, so he wasn't all bad. It became popular with the Connaught Rangers in World War I, and was soon being sung by the entire British Army, which unfortunately kept giving away their positions to the Germans.

SADLY, THE SWEETEST GIRL PADDY KNEW PUT A FEW POUNDS ON WHILE HE WAS AWAY AT THE FRONT

John Hinde Postcards

John Hinde did for the image of Ireland on postcards what *The Quiet Man* had achieved in the movies – created a world as unreal as an Irish property developer's tax return. If you got a John Hinde postcard you would be convinced that the sun shone every day of the year in Ireland, that we all lived in pretty, thatched, whitewashed cottages amid beautiful scenery, and that the flowers were always in bloom and the locals always full of the joys of spring. Oh, and we were all coppertops and gingernuts (redheads to you).

Apparently, old John used to go around with a saw to cut down any inconvenient trees that

JAYSUS, I HOPE HE DOESN'T RETOUCH ME RED AS WELL.

got in the way of his shots, would drop in the odd bit of azure Caribbean sea to brighten up the murky grey Atlantic, and ask kids and men driving carts to change their clothes so they looked more like 'the real thing'.

His most famous shot is of a boy and girl in Connemara loading turf into baskets on the back of a donkey. The kids' hair is so red it looks like they've been fed on rusty nails all their lives and then had their hair dyed with whore-red industrial paint. Still, s'pose anything's better than the reality...

The Land of Saints and Scholars

You probably recall some teacher telling you that Ireland was once known as The Land of Saints and Scholars, and if you're old enough, you can probably remember some Christian Brother kicking the shite out of you to help you remember it.

The reason we earned this worthy title was that in the 5th to 8th centuries Ireland had a great monastic tradition, i.e. lots of monks working like the clappers producing manuscripts like the Book of Kells. These monasteries

THE GREAT SEAT OF LEARNING AT
GLENDALOUGH DURING RAG WEEK.

were like universities today – no, not full of
drug-addled, spotty youths – but great seats of
learning. And many of our monks legged it to
Europe where they founded more monasteries
all over the gaff. As Europe was in the Dark
Ages, these holy, learned men were seen as
beacons of knowledge and understanding, thus
the nifty nickname.

Nowadays of course, thanks to the monks'
successors (the Catholic Church) and state
corruption, Ireland is now the one in the Dark
Ages.

The Leprechaun

According to legend, the leprechaun is a type of fairy (see also *Irish Fairies*) who takes the form of a three-foot tall old man and who enjoys mischief-making.

The leprechaun wears a red — not green — coat and makes shoes for a living, he enjoys playing music and drinking poteen and when he's not on the batter he sits at the end of a rainbow, counting his gold. If you manage to catch a leprechaun (difficult) he will grant you three wishes. It is often given as proof that leprechauns don't exist that 1) Ireland has never won the World Cup 2) No banker has ever gone to jail 3) It buckets rain for three months every summer.

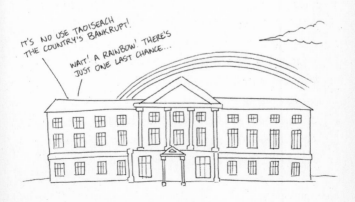

Ireland's first National Leprechaun Museum has opened in Dublin, and recently the EU made an area in the Cooley Mountains, County Louth an 'official designated area for the Protection of the Little People', citing the fact that they were concerned 'about the continuing deterioration of natural habitats posed to *certain species*'. Not coddin' you.

On reflection, why did we ever join the EU?

Oirish *(See also Begorrah)*

Oirish is a mythical language that for some reason (mostly Brit & Yank TV & movies) much of the world thinks we actually speak on this island. It includes terms like 'top o' de mornin' and a multitude of other words and phrases that may have once existed, but have been obsolete for over a century. 'Top of the mornin' for example, has long since been replaced with 'Howaya, ye bollix ye.' Anyway, a typical sentence spoken in Oirish would go something like this:

'Top o' de mornin', Seamus. D'ye know what, begob, I was just tinkin' on dis fine soft day dat soft words butter no parsnips but they

won't harden the heart of de cabbage aither.
Now dat's a fact, bay de hokey.'

Pictures over the Mantelpiece.

Up to the 1970s, 100% of Irish Catholic homes had the following three items over the mantelpiece: A plate bearing a picture of JFK, a plate bearing a picture of the Pope, a large picture of the Sacred Heart with a little red light shining in front of it.

If you were discovered not to have any of these items the bishop would send around the local Garda sergeant who would proceed to kick the living shite out of you.

Pig in the Parlour

The Pig in the Parlour is another invention of our friends across the water, an image originally created in the mid-nineteenth century to portray the Irish as a bunch of ignorant muck savages who shared their homes with farm animals and pigshite, but one they tried to maintain until recent years.

The reality is quite the reverse, as the English to this day not only keep pigs in their parlours but also in their kitchens, bedrooms, bathrooms etc. They also keep cows, chickens and various other farm animals. On top of all that, most English people can't read or write, they drink excessively and get plastered after two 'alves of lager. When they eat, they use their hands, as the knife and fork is beyond their intelligence. They are also all a bunch of wimps and most of the men wear panties!

Now, let's see if that bit of invented propaganda sticks as long as the other.

[And, of course, we're only kidding. English people do use knives and forks.]

58

Pint of Stout

Roughly one million pints of stout are consumed every day in Ireland, and that's just by the politicians in the Dáil Bar. Since it became the 'national drink' a couple of hundred years ago, we've been doing our patriotic best to guzzle as much of the stuff as humanly possible without falling over. It has been a source of joy, misery, craic, pain, acting the maggot, sealing the deal, getting the leg over and getting legless. It is loved equally by slappers, sleeveens, cute hoors and gobshites, holy Joes, mucksavages and jackeens.

You may be interested to know that it is made from water, hops, barley and brewer's yeast and is treated with isinglass finings which are made from fishes' bladders. Maybe that's why it makes you run to the jacks every twenty minutes?

Poteen

This famed illicit drink is one of the most potent beverages in the world, i.e. it could strip the lining off a wild goat's stomach. In fact it was once under consideration by the chemical weapons proliferation committee. A couple of firms now make poteen legally, and a couple of hundred gougers still make it illegally.

Traditional poteen was made from potatoes and was usually 90-95% proof, which is sufficiently potent to render most people paralytic after a couple of mouthfuls. If poorly made, illicit poteen can contain large amounts of methanol, which at best will blind you and at worst will put you in a wooden box.

It was very popular at wakes as someone usually keeled over stone dead from the stuff, which meant they could have another wake.

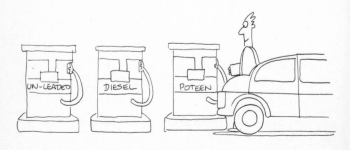

Red Hair

If you were to believe the movies and books, half the feckin' country are flaming coppertops. Ireland does produce lots of redsers – about 10% of the total population. But the Scots are actually

JAYSUS... ALL I ASKED WAS IF SHE WAS AS RED DOWN SOUTH AS SHE IS UP NORTH...

the world carrothead champions, with 13% of the Jockos walking around with a rusty mop on top.

If you're a 'traditional Irish redhead' you may be interested to know that your tomato head means you've got two copies of a recessive gene on chromosome 16 and your hair is full of the pigment pheomelanin. That'll teach you to ask.

Irish gingernuts are also supposed to have a fiery temperament and a sharp tongue (e.g. Maureen O'Hara in *The Quiet Man*), are more sensitive to pain and are as randy as a rabbit on Viagra.

Round Tower

Most Irish people were taught that Ireland's round towers were built so that the monks could leg it up inside them to hide when the Vikings came pillaging and raping over the hill. And some of the poor gobdaws actually tried this, at which point the cute Vikings sleeveens would light a fire around the bottom and suffocate everyone inside.

In actual fact, the towers were built as belfries so that the monks could clatter their bell and

WHAT DO YOU MEAN, YOU NEVER PUT IN A FIRE EXIT?!?

summon everyone around to come and attend a four-hour mass in Latin, which was almost as bad a fate as being pillaged and raped by a Viking horde.

The tallest of these monuments from ancient times is 40 metres high and there are still about twenty complete towers remaining, so the government is formulating plans to re-direct a motorway through them or re-zone the land they're on for office space.

Shamrock

The ultimate Irish cliché, as Irish as spaghetti is Italian or scoring from an illegal hand ball is French, the shamrock is one of Ireland's national symbols, along with the harp, the tricolour, the Irish wolfhound, the pint of stout, the Celtic cross etc etc etc.

St Patrick used the shamrock (three-leafed clover) to explain the Holy Trinity, or so the story goes, but that's probably a pile of horse-shite. But, like horseshite, the story stuck and we've been wearing the stuff on St Patrick's Day for donkey's years. Well, actually, most people either can't be arsed wearing any at

all or wear a plastic shamrock badge that was made in China.

Traditionally, the Taoiseach presents the President of the US with a bowl of shamrock on Paddy's Day, which the President immediately dumps in the trashcan the moment he's managed to get the Taoiseach out the White House gates.

 Shillelagh

The famous Irish blackthorn stick harks back to a centuries-old Irish tradition of batin' the living shite out of the English, not to mention each other. Made from blackthorn and about the same length as a walking stick, the wood was smeared with butter and left up the chimney, which blackened and hardened it, making it much more effective at bashing in one's opponents' brains. Enthusiasts would also hollow out the 'hammer' end and fill it with lead, which increased the depth that the weapon would sink into some poor eejit's skull.

It became popular in the nineteenth century among agrarian gangs who found its brain-pulping qualities an effective deterrent against English landlords. It was also often used in Irish faction fights, which took place at county fairs, funerals, weddings etc, and involved a gansey-load of fluthered men and women laying into each other with their favourite shillelagh. This

added to the general fun and bonhomie of the occasion. This fine custom was called '*bataireacht*'.

In fact, the shillelagh was so effective at penetrating the skull that the American army named an anti-tank missile after it, called the MGM-51 Shillelagh. Ah, the depth of our cultural heritage knows no end.

St Brigid's Cross

This is another of those unofficial symbols of Ireland, like the old lady on the hospital trolley.

The cross is made by interweaving rushes or straw, producing a square in the centre with four arms projecting out, a task not to be attempted when you've just come back from the local having guzzled thirteen pints.

It apparently originated when a pagan in Kildare was about to kick the bucket and St Brigid was called to have a last gasp try at converting him. As she sat by his bedside she picked up straw from the floor and began to weave a cross. The poor gobshite was so bored watching this that he agreed to be baptised so he could croak it and be put out of his misery.

For centuries now it has been said that the cross, when hung over the hearth, will ward off fire, evil and telesales people.

St Patrick

St Patrick was English – let's get that unsavoury fact out of the way. He was captured by Irish raiders around the fifth century, back in the good old days when we used to go over there and kick the shite out of them, rather than the other way round. He was sixteen at the time and was kept as a slave for six years in

ST PATRICK BANISHED US FROM IRELAND

LUCKY BASTARD.

County Antrim before he managed to leg it back home. There he had a vision from God telling him to go back and convert the greedy, power-hungry Irish shower of savages to Christianity, which he did with most of the people, omitting to convert the politicians, bankers, county councillors and property developers, who remain a greedy, power-hungry shower of savages to this day.

Legend has it that he fasted for forty days and nights on Croagh Patrick, after which he banished the snakes from Ireland, which was a piece of cake, really, as there were no snakes in post-glacial Ireland.

His life is celebrated every year on 17 March, which is, ironically, the day he kicked the bucket. The celebrations involve every town in Ireland organizing a huge parade of the locals, which generally heads straight for the nearest pub and stays there until they've 'drowned the shamrock', in other words, become bollixed drunk.

Tara

The Hill of Tara was once the seat of the High Kings of Ireland, or at the very least the site of the High King's inauguration hooley. It is likely that all the key decisions regarding the rule of Ireland were made here, as opposed to in a pub in Baggot Street, Dublin, where they are made today.

Some of the monuments and artefacts on Tara date to around 3000BC and it was still associated with the ancient Irish monarchy until the Brits arrived in AD1169 and made a hames of everything. All that remains of the great forts that once stood on the hill are a number of circular mounds in the earth. At the centre of one of these stands the Lia Fáil, or Stone of Destiny, which was said to sing

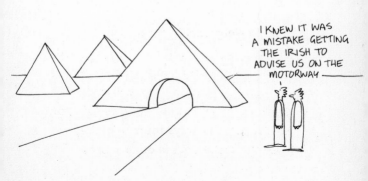

I KNEW IT WAS A MISTAKE GETTING THE IRISH TO ADVISE US ON THE MOTORWAY

when touched by the true king, usually giving a rousing rendition of 'The Fields of Athenry'.

At the start of the 20th century, a bunch of British Israelites started digging up the hill because they thought the Ark of the Covenant was buried there *[Mother of Jaysus!]*. More recently, another nutter decided to vandalize the broader area, which contains gansey-loads of archaeological treasures, by building a motorway just a couple of kilometers away. This particular gobshite was called the Minister for Transport.

The Thatched Cottage

Once upon a time about half the population of Ireland lived in thatched cottages, although they weren't quite the quaint little homesteads we stick on our postcards, as they usually had only one room, there was no jacks, and all hanky panky had to be done under the gaze of the rest of the family, which normally numbered about twenty-six children.

The thatch was made from rushes or heather and the stone was often whitewashed to protect it and to prettify its appearance. This style of building mostly died out in Ireland

when it was replaced by millions of bungalows
of the Doric-Romanesque-Victorian-Baroque-
Edwardian-Gothic-Tudor style, an effect which
could be achieved by using stick-on bricks,
hollow plastic columns, fake cross-beams and
about three tons of hideous taste.

The Wake

In Ireland we've never been short of excuses
to have a party, and one of the most popular
used to be when some unfortunate head-the-
ball kicked the bucket. No sooner had poor
Seamus or Mary croaked their last breath,
than a session could begin in earnest.

After the women had washed and dressed
the body, the stiff would traditionally be
slapped up on the kitchen table with a set of

rosary beads in his/her hands. Then everyone would take turns to say a prayer over the deceased, and, that nasty business out of the way, immediately begin to toast the departed and exchange funny stories about what a wonderful soul he/she was, even if he/she was the most conniving sleeveen that ever walked the earth. The merriment would often be accompanied by keening, which involved a couple of wrinkly old bags screeching like a pig with its arse on fire, until the spirit left the body through an open window, which it was probably desperate to do, given the bleedin' racket in the house.

Ah, God be with the ould days!

The Wolfhound

The world's tallest breed of dog, the iconic Irish wolfhound is so huge that the ancient Romans even paraded them around the Coliseum as a support act before they got on with the main business of feeding Christians to the lions.

They've been in Ireland since at least 3000BC and, surprise, surprise, they were originally used to hunt wolves. They were also trained to attack English knights and pull

them from their horses so that they could be safely bludgeoned to a pulp. But despite their size (up to two metres on hind legs) and their strength, the modern breed of wolfhound is about as fierce as an oul' wan of ninety.

Ironically, it was thanks to an Englishman that the breed, which was almost extinct by the mid-nineteenth century, survived. George Graham began a breeding program, allowing the Irish Wolfhounds to indulge in a quickie or two with some Great Danes, resulting in the dog we know today.

Because of the mild temperament of this modern breed, as watchdogs they're as useful as a concrete currach.

 # The Yoke

Unique to the Irish, the word 'yoke' is remarkable in its flexibility. Most foreigners translate 'yoke' as 'thing', but it is much more than that. A yoke *can* be a thing – 'Hey, head the ball, givvus a hand with this yoke,' or 'where's that yoke for changing the channels?'

But it can also refer to a person, usually in a derogatory way – 'You didn't sleep with that useless yoke, did ye?' It can be used as a compliment – 'Jaysus, your wan's got a fine pair of yokes on her.' It can refer to foodstuffs – 'That yoke I ate last night gave me the scutters.' Or it can be used during courting rituals – 'That's the smallest yoke I've ever seen.'

And it can also form the basis of entire conversations:

> 'What's that yoke?'
> 'This yoke? It's a yoke for doing stuff with the other yoke.'
> 'Did that yoke Deirdre give it to ye?'
> 'No, her friend, the one who wears the see-through yokes.'
> 'She's a right yoke, that wan.'
> 'Yeah, she gives a great yoke as well.'

Makes perfect sense to all us Irish yokes.

Colin Murphy

Donal O'Dea

Colin Murphy & **Donal O'Dea** are the co-authors of fourteen hugely successful Feckin' books which deal with yokes as diverse as Irish Slang, Sex, Sayings, History, Insults and Trivia, to mention but a few. Now they've turned their attention to the many wojus clichés with which Ireland has become associated down the years. Having both grown up in households that sported the St Brigid's Cross, pictures of the Sacred Heart and JFK over the mantelpiece and lumps of Connemara marble in every nook and cranny, they are utterly familiar with Ireland's sometimes tacky, often hilarious iconography, although they do confess to having a weakness for comely maidens, full Irish breakfasts and all of the alcohol-related Irish clichés.

Colin is married to Grainne and they have a couple of grown up childer, all of whom have red hair and love Irish stew and playing the harp. Donal is married to Karen and they have three childer, all of whom also have rusty red hair, play the fiddle and carry shillelaghs with them everywhere. Colin and Donal both hail from the world of advertising, although Colin left it behind a couple of years ago so he could devote more time to céilí dancing. Donal spends most of his spare time hunting leprechauns in the Cooley Mountains.

*Some more hilarious Books in the
Feckin' Collection*

The Feckin' Book of **Bankers, Builders, Blaggers and other Bowsies** who banjaxed the nation

The Feckin' Book of **Irish History** for anyone who hasn't been paying attention for the last 30,000 years

The book of feckin' **Irish Slang** that's great craic for cute hoors and bowsies

The book of deadly **Irish Quotations** some smart fecker in the pub is always blatherin' on about

The book of **Irish Songs** yer oul' fella always sang when he was jarred at a hooley

Now That's what I Call a Big Feckin' Irish Book: Jammers with Insults, Proverbs, Family Names, Trivia, Slang

Also from the bestselling team of Colin Murphy and Donal O'Dea:
STUFF IRISH PEOPLE LOVE:
The Definitive Guide to the Unique Passions of the Paddies

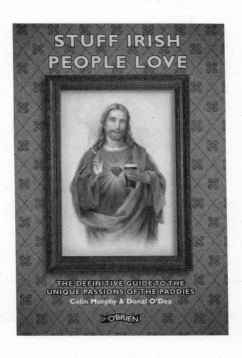

www.obrien.ie